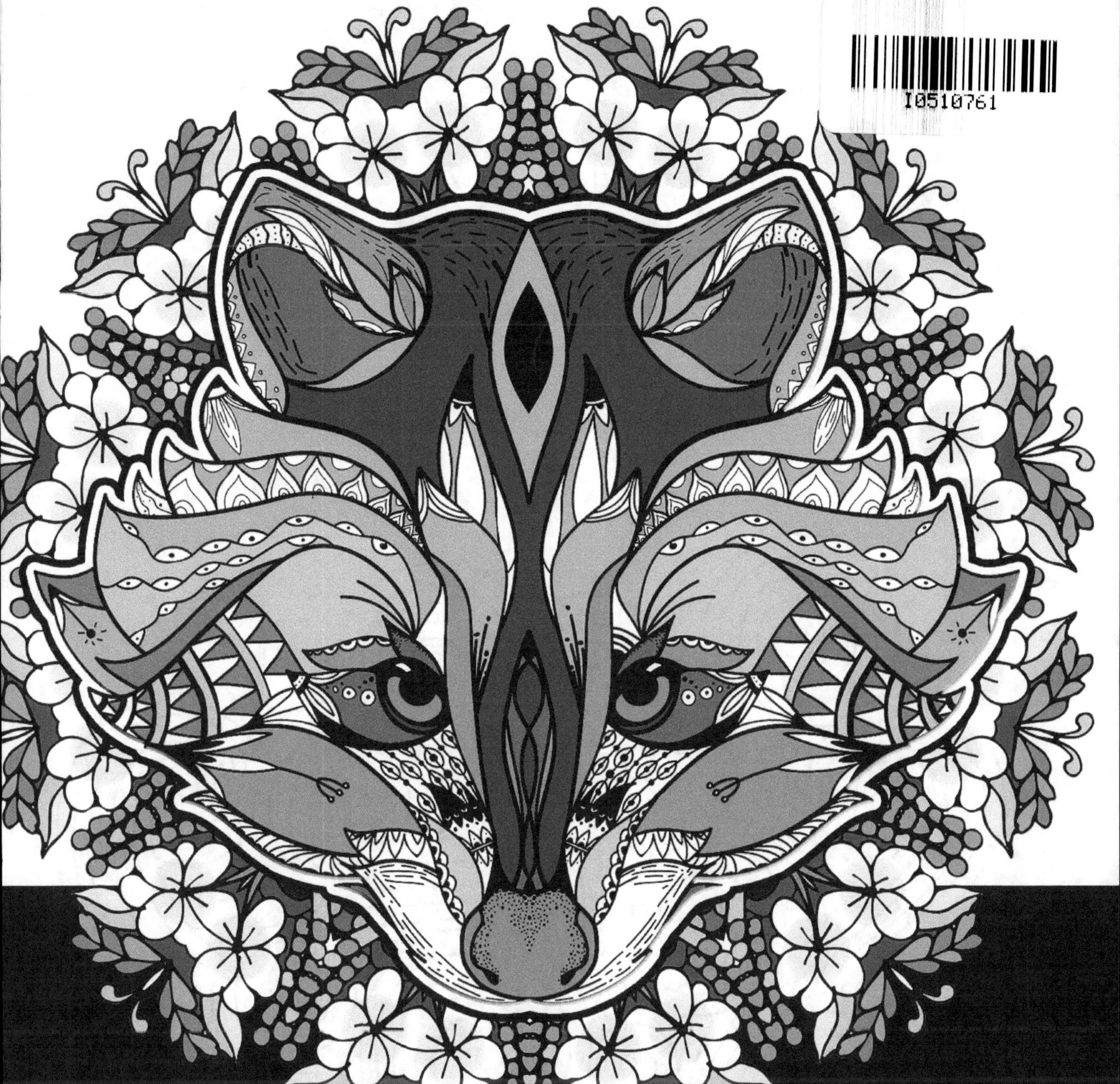

Raccoon

and Mandalas

COLORING BOOK FOR ADULTS

AMAZING DESIGNS

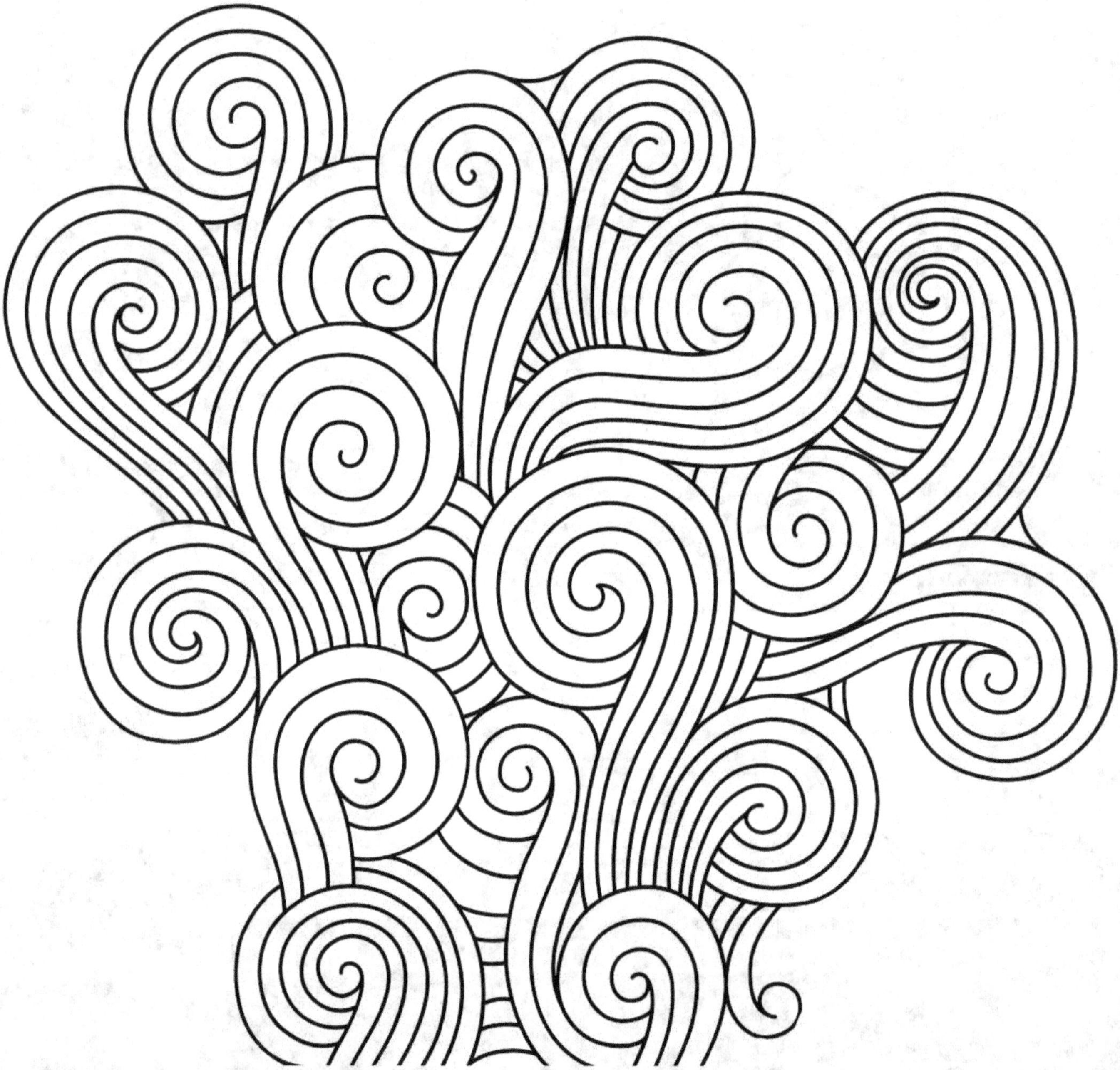

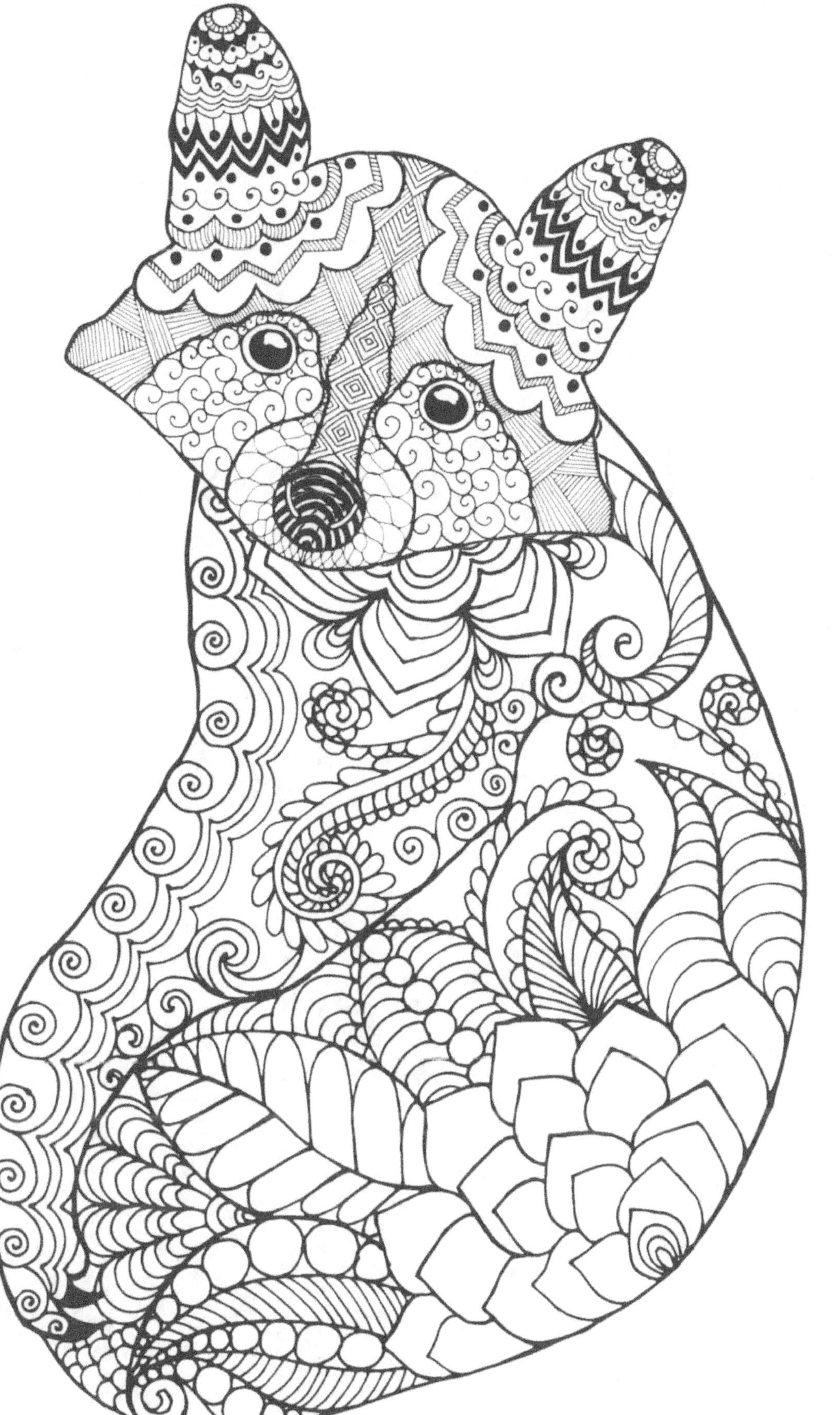

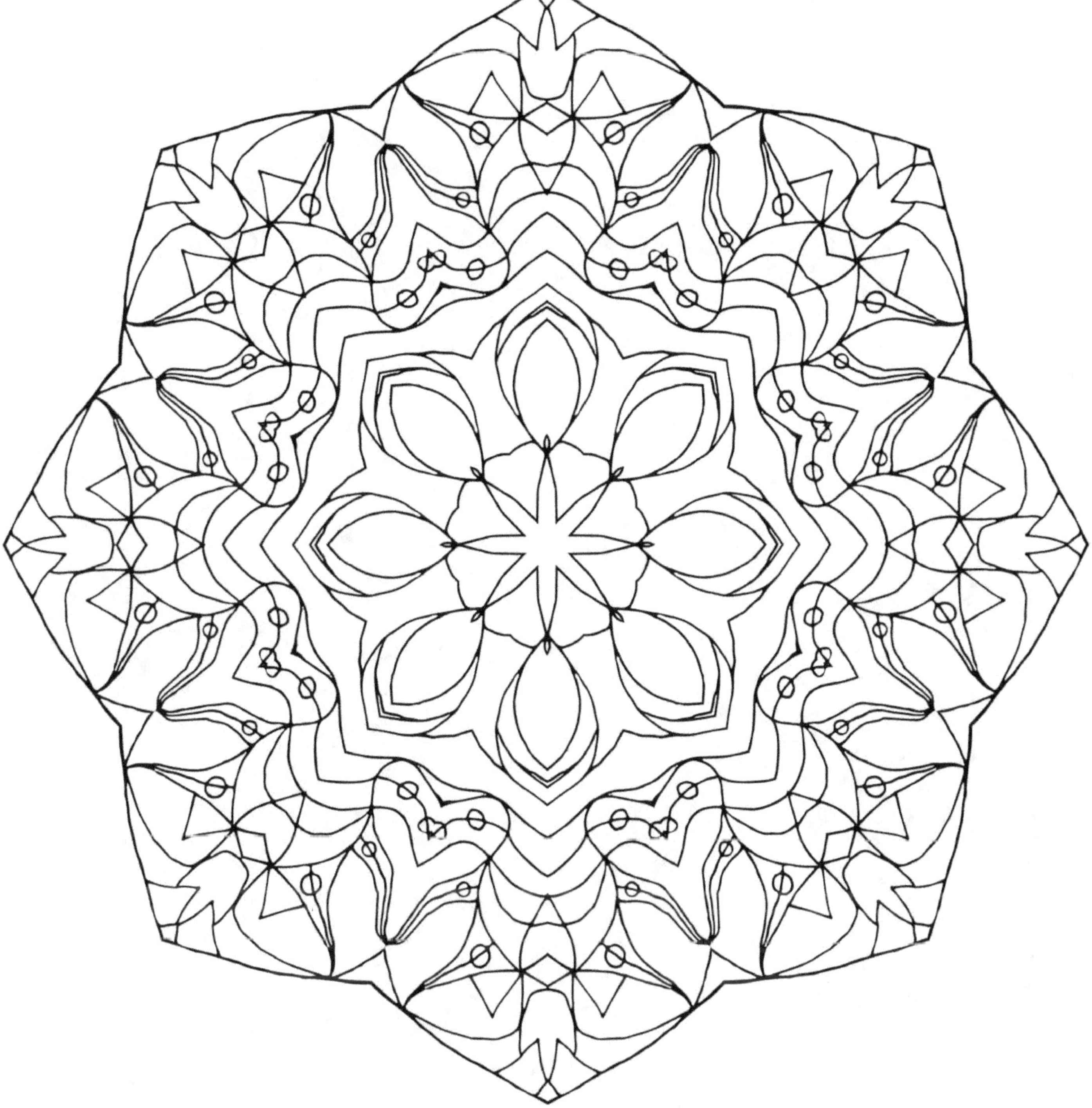

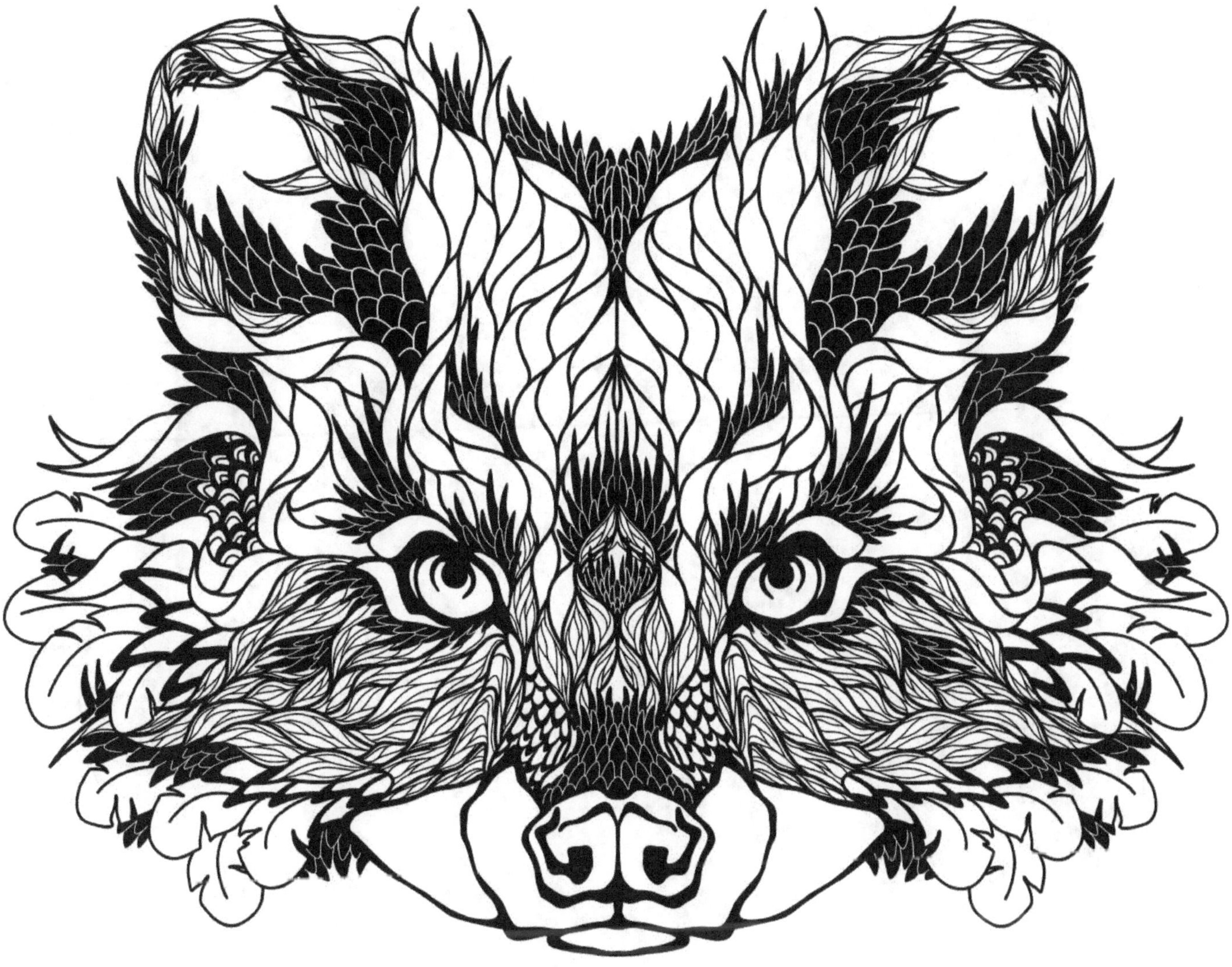

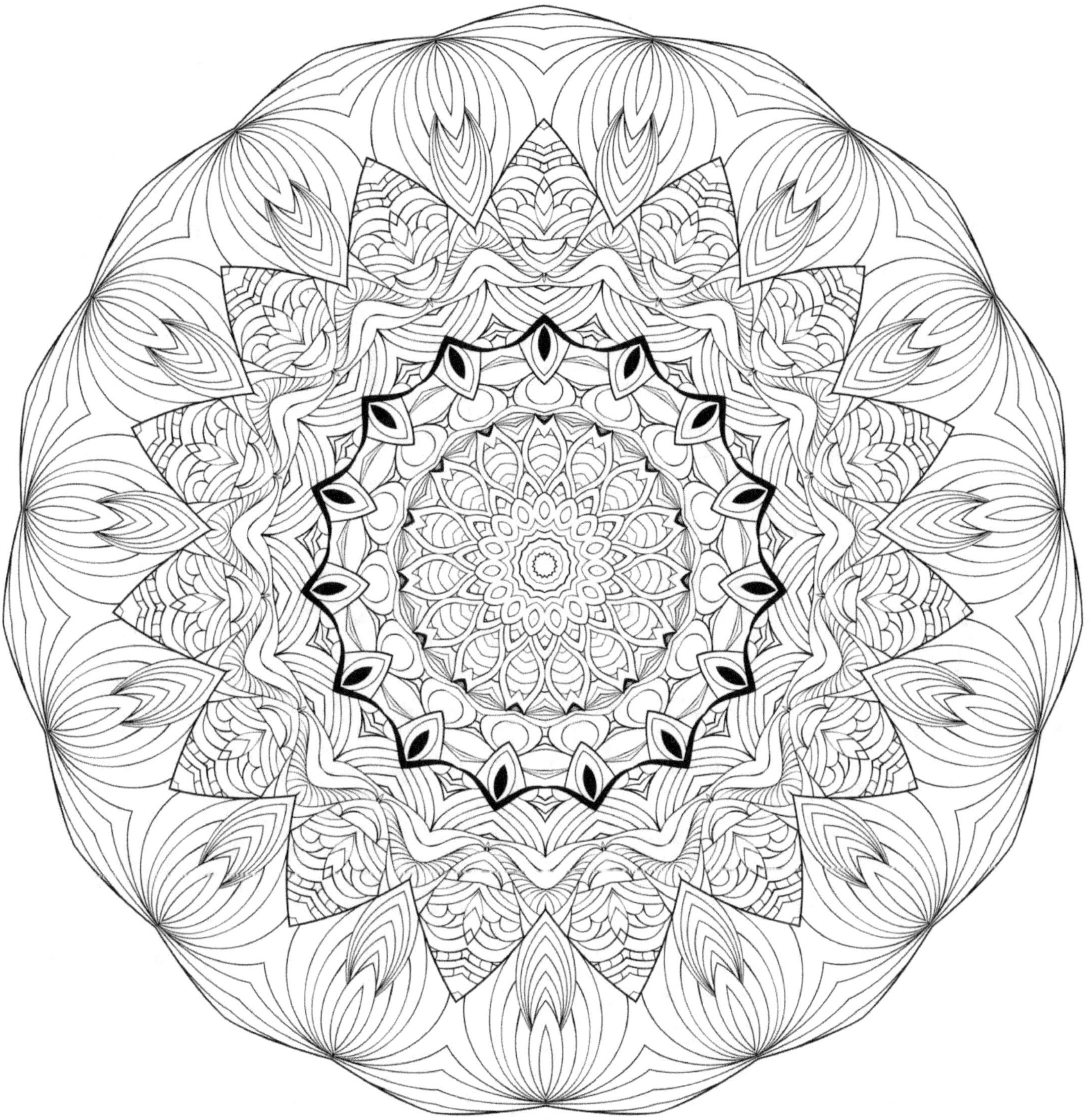

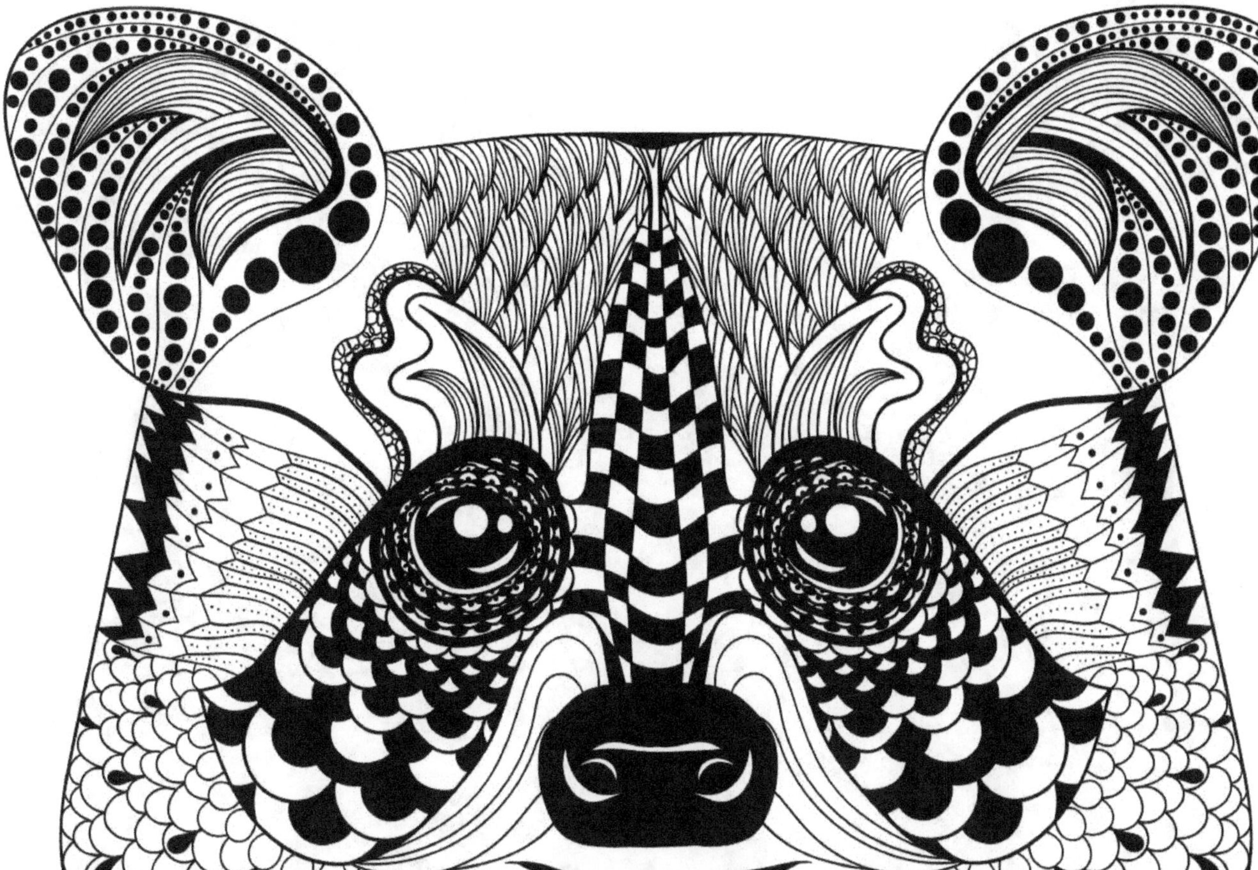

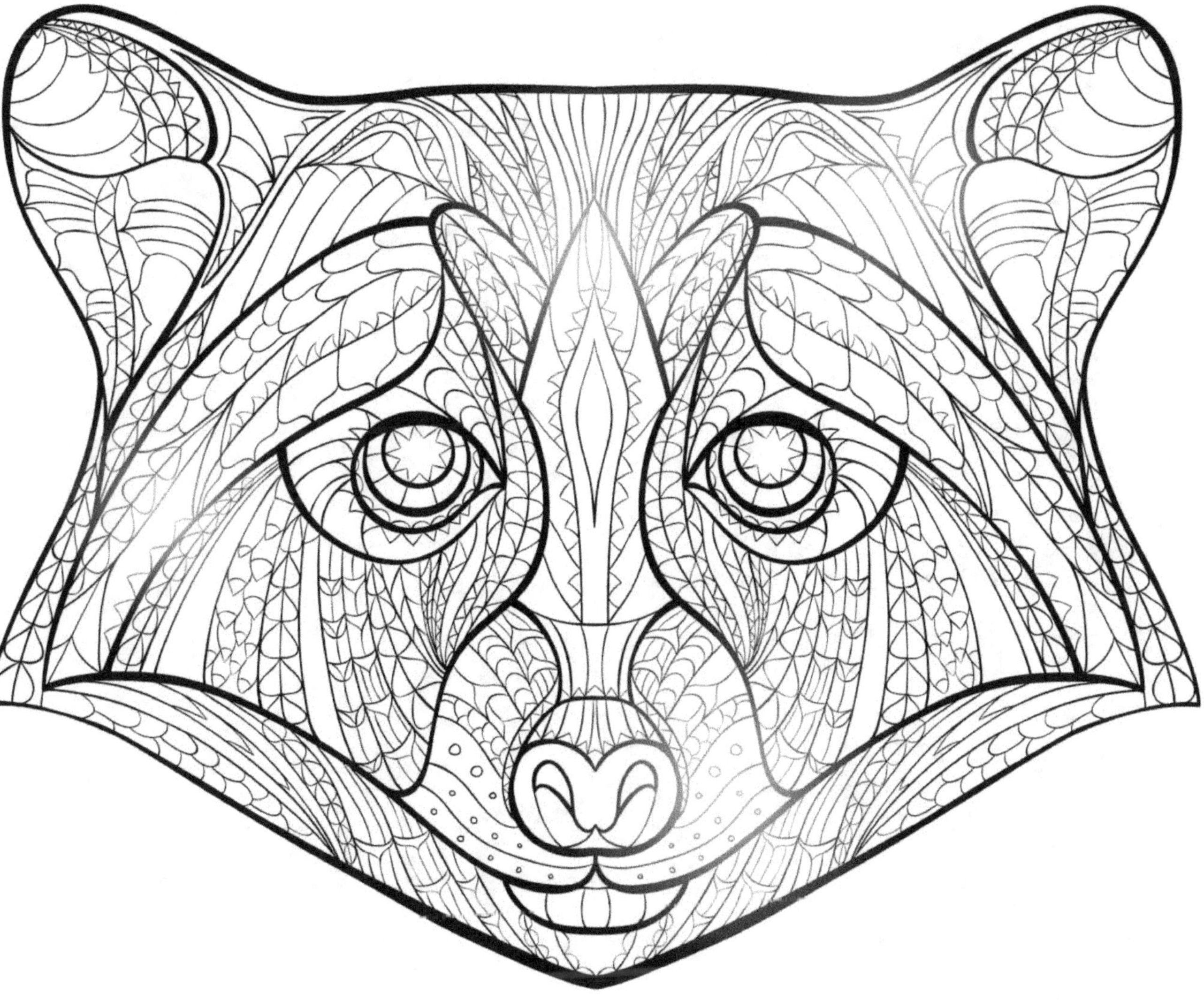

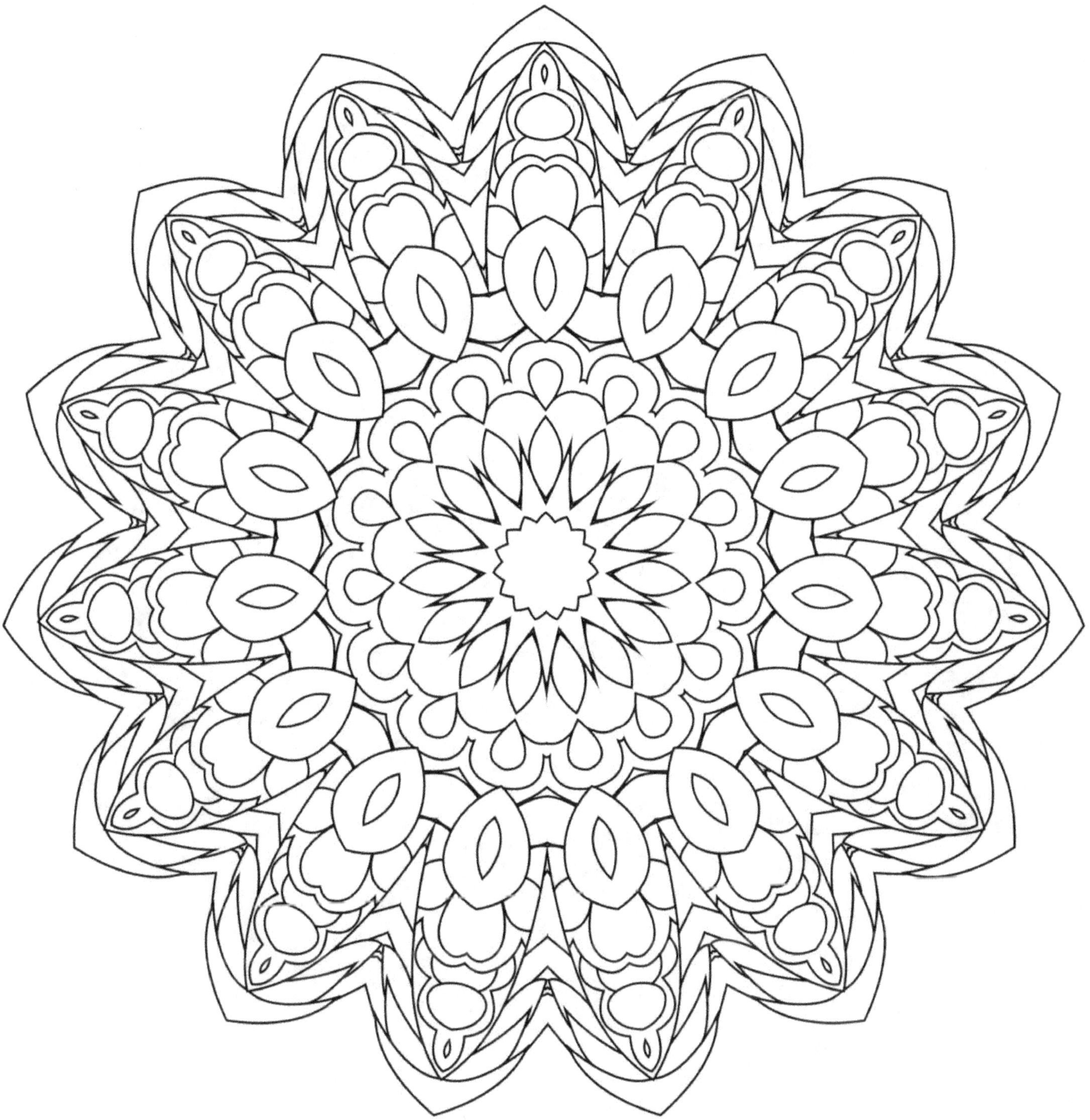

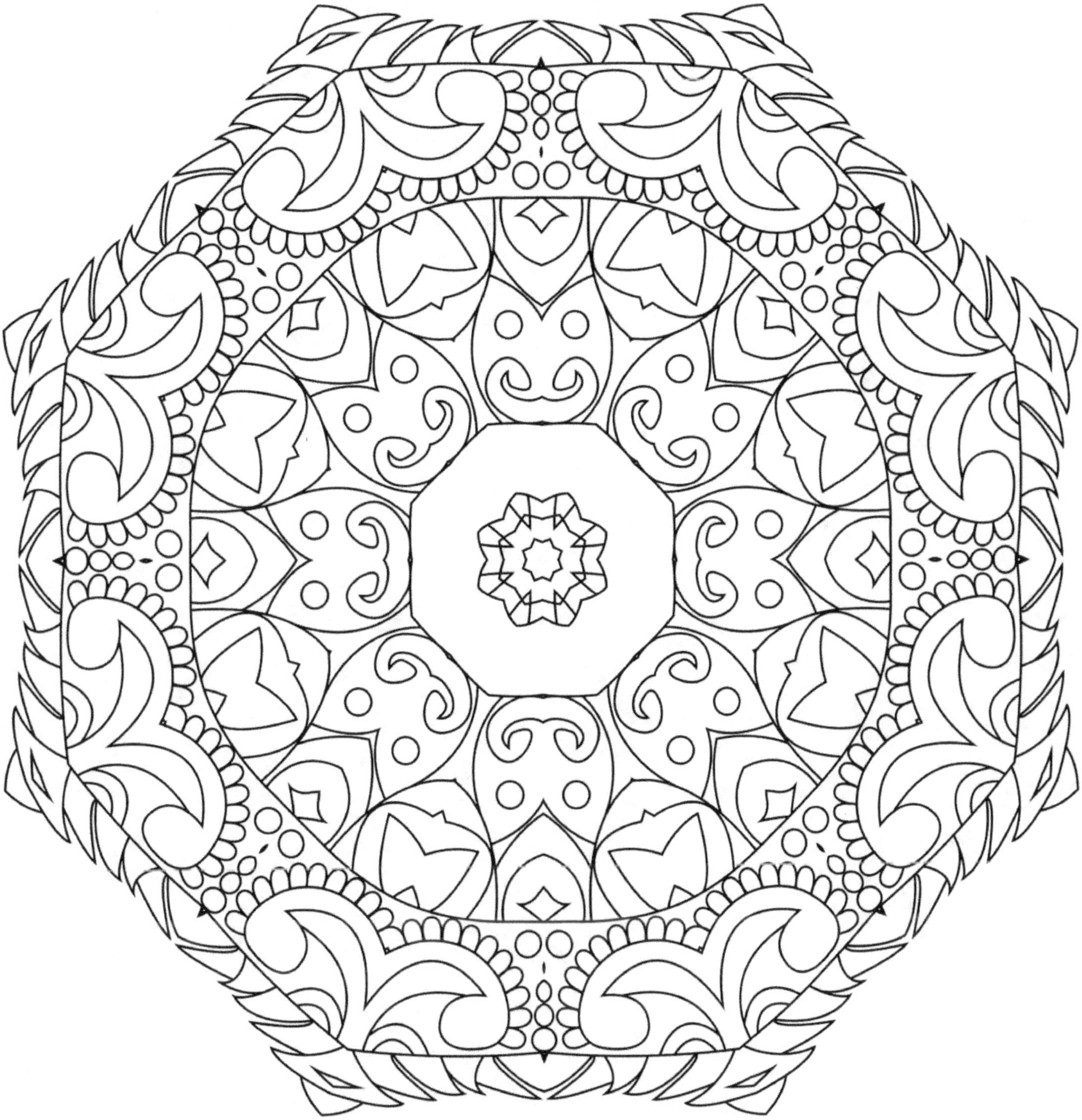

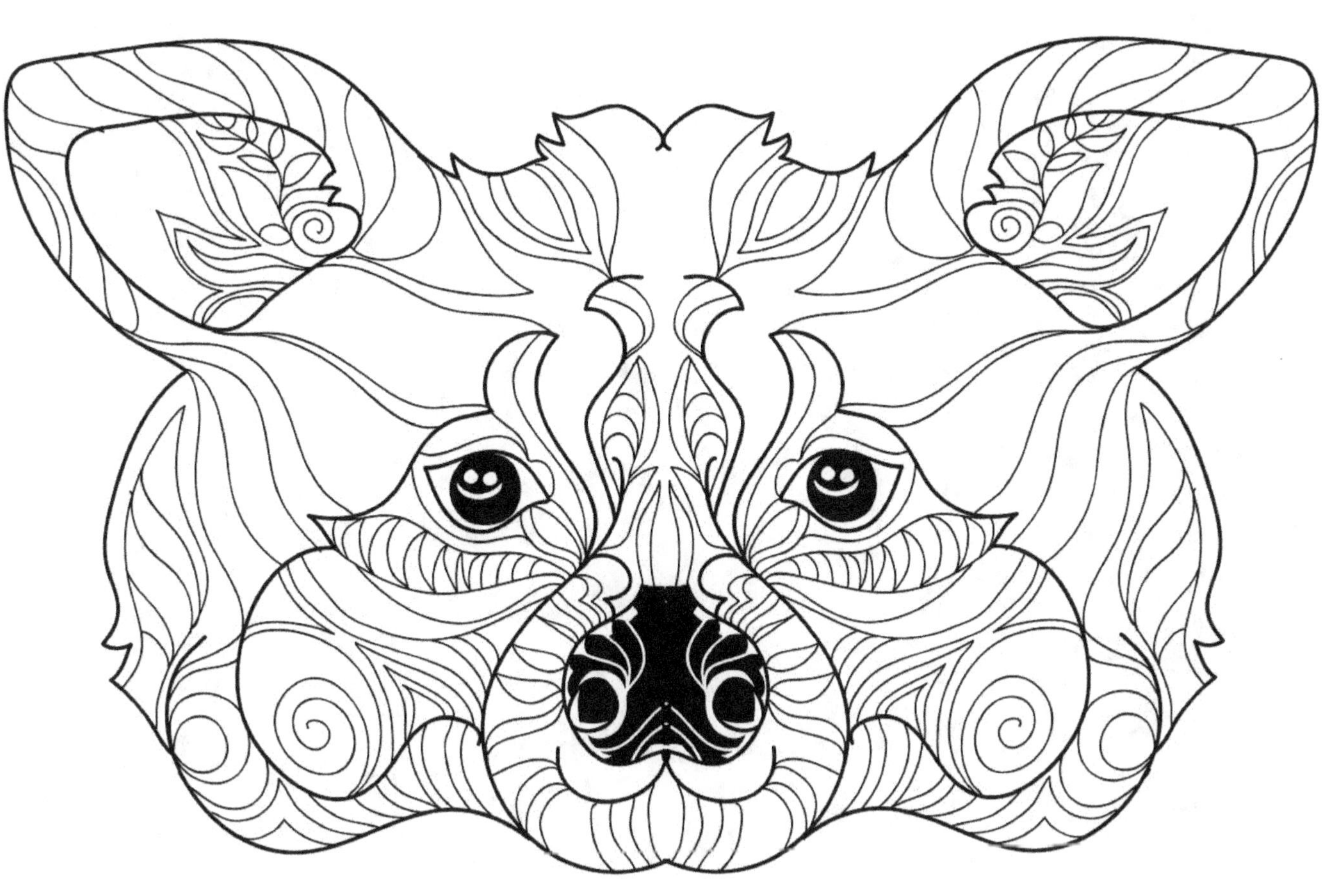

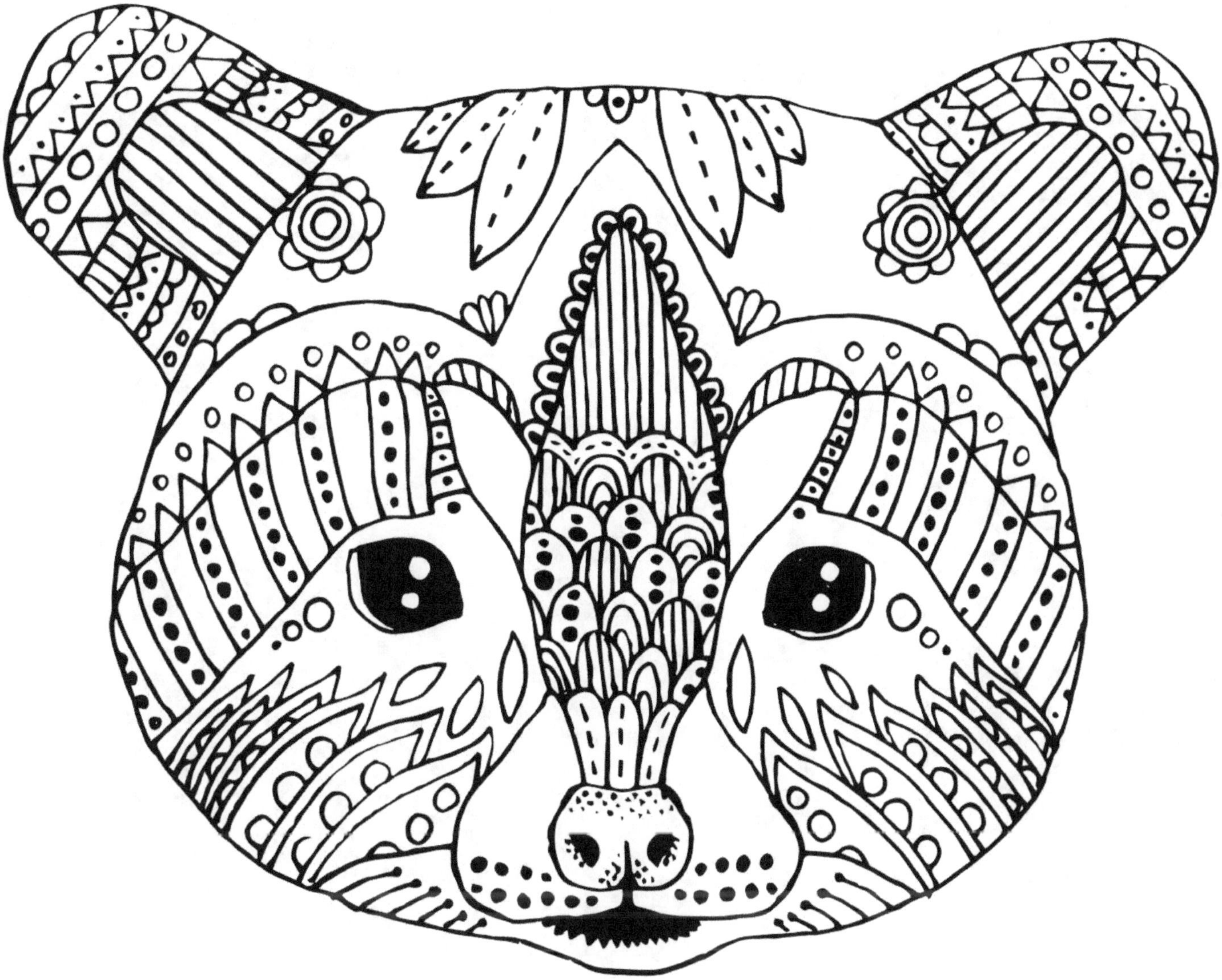

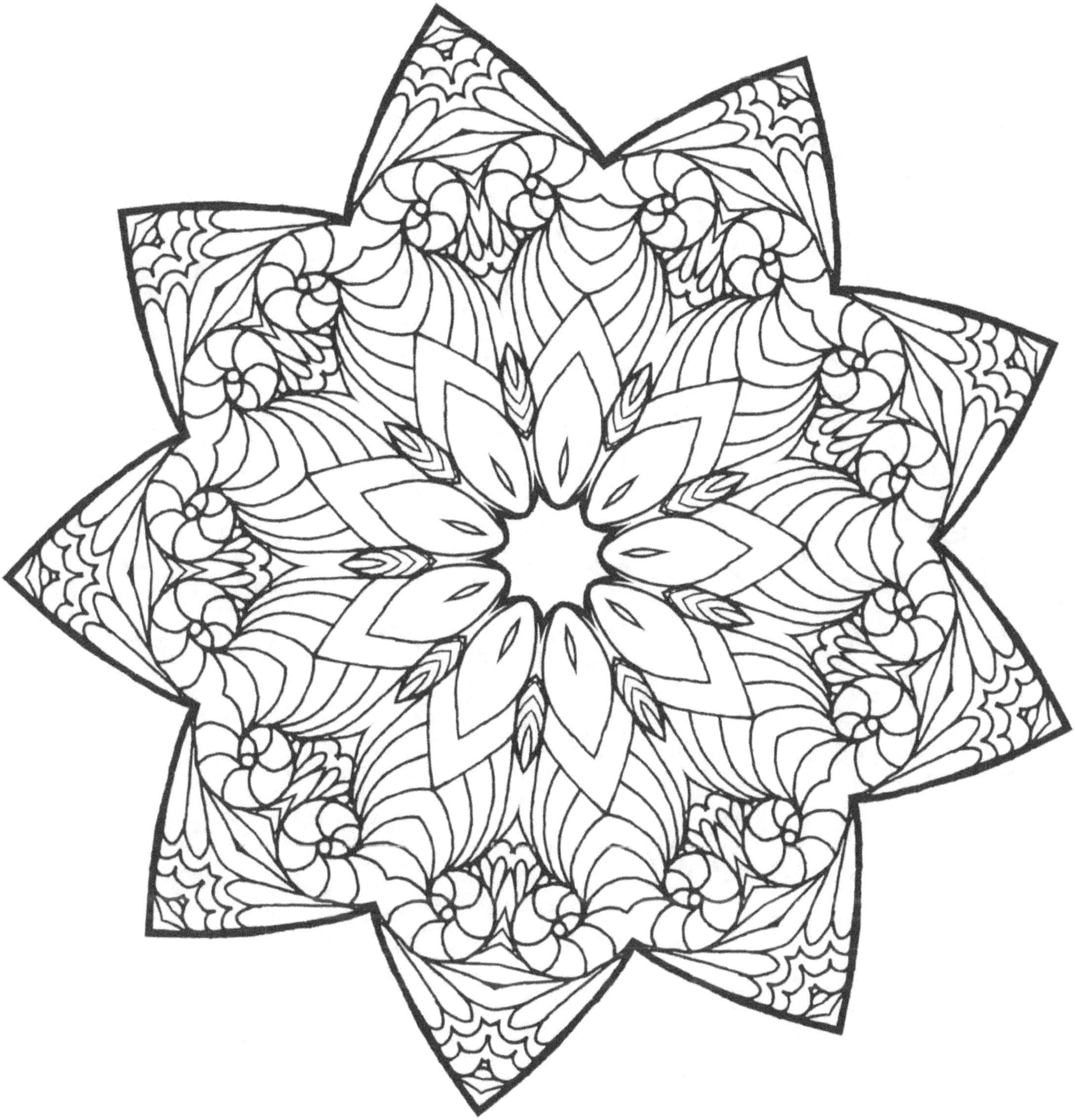

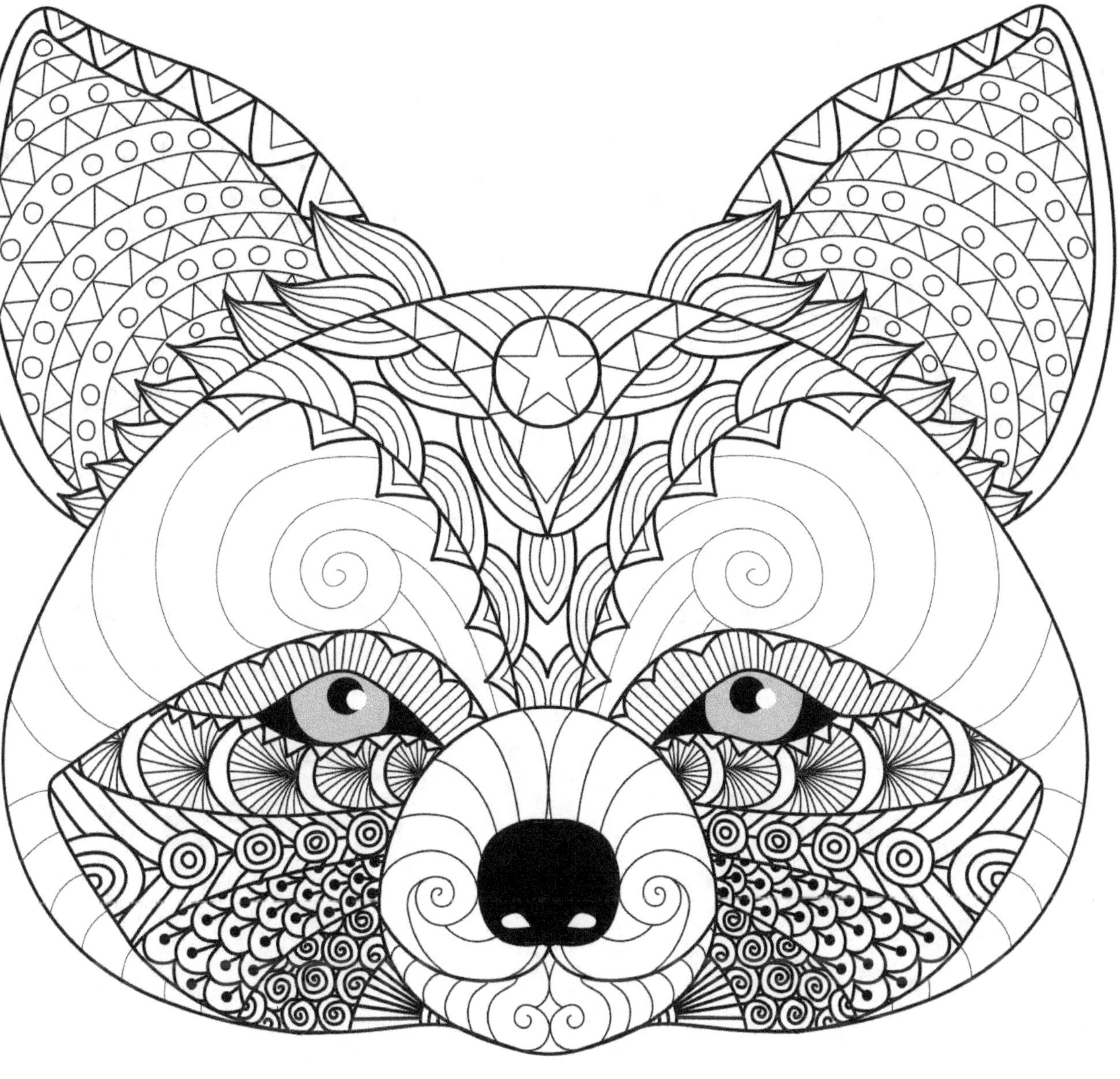

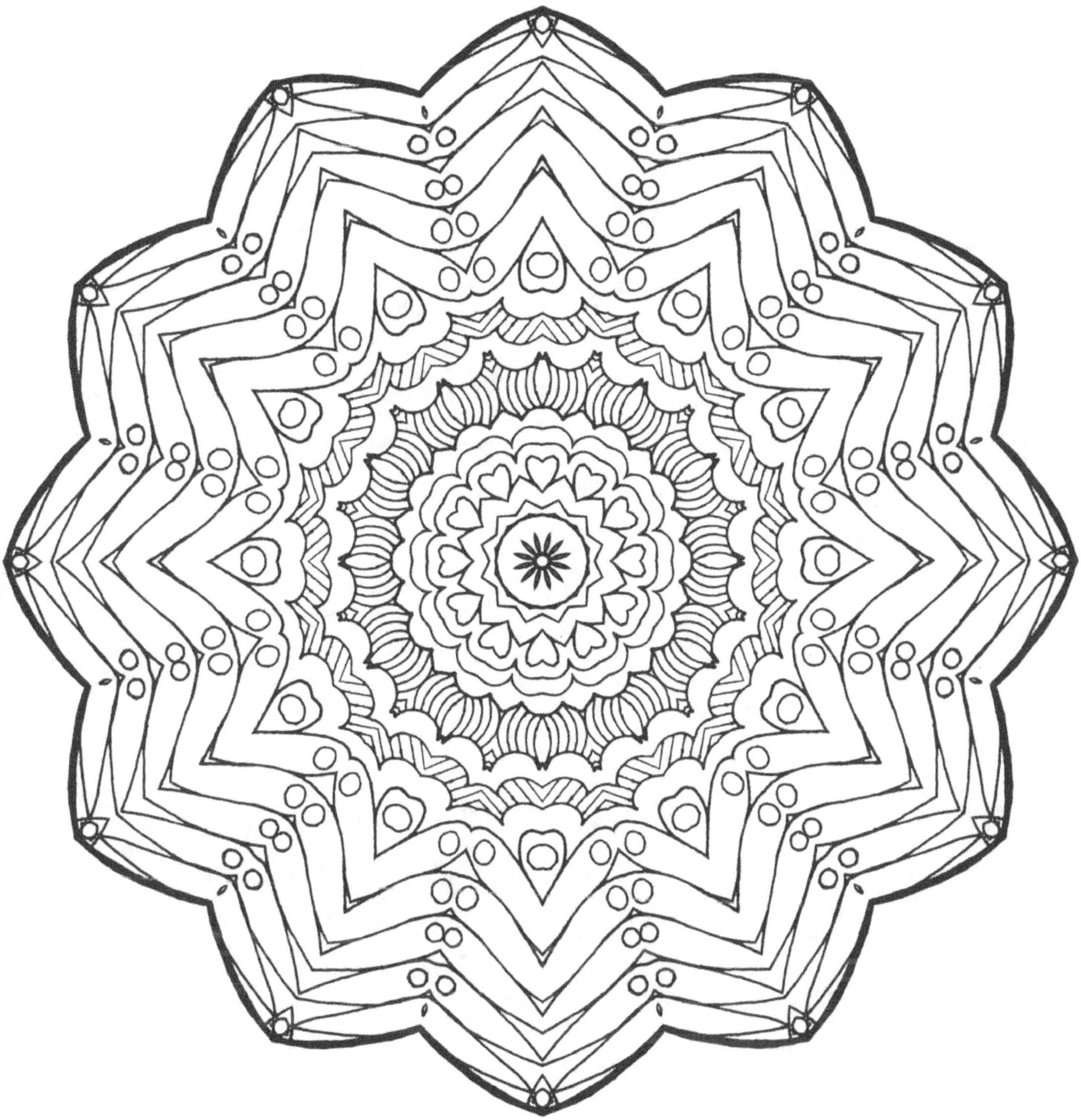

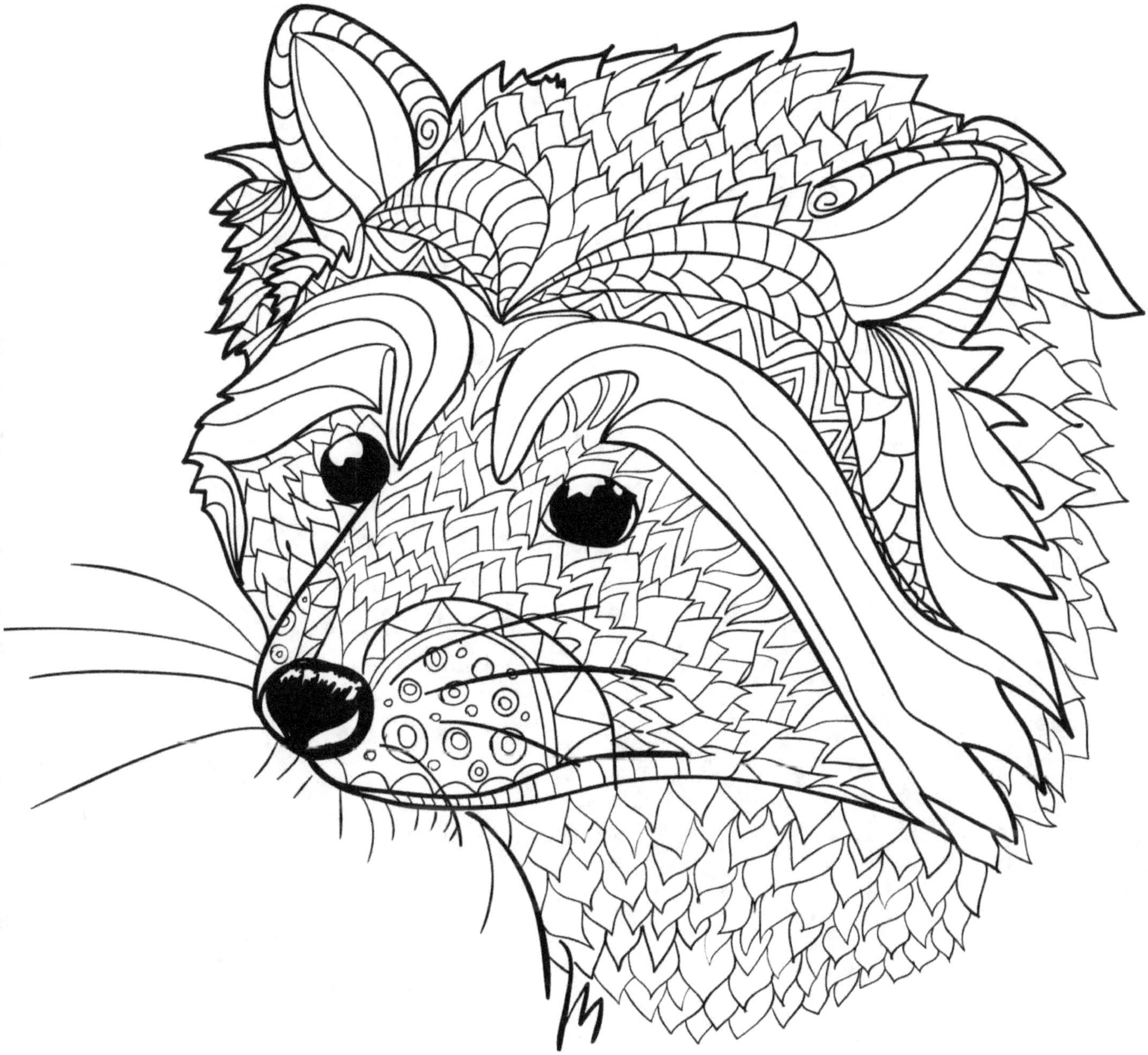

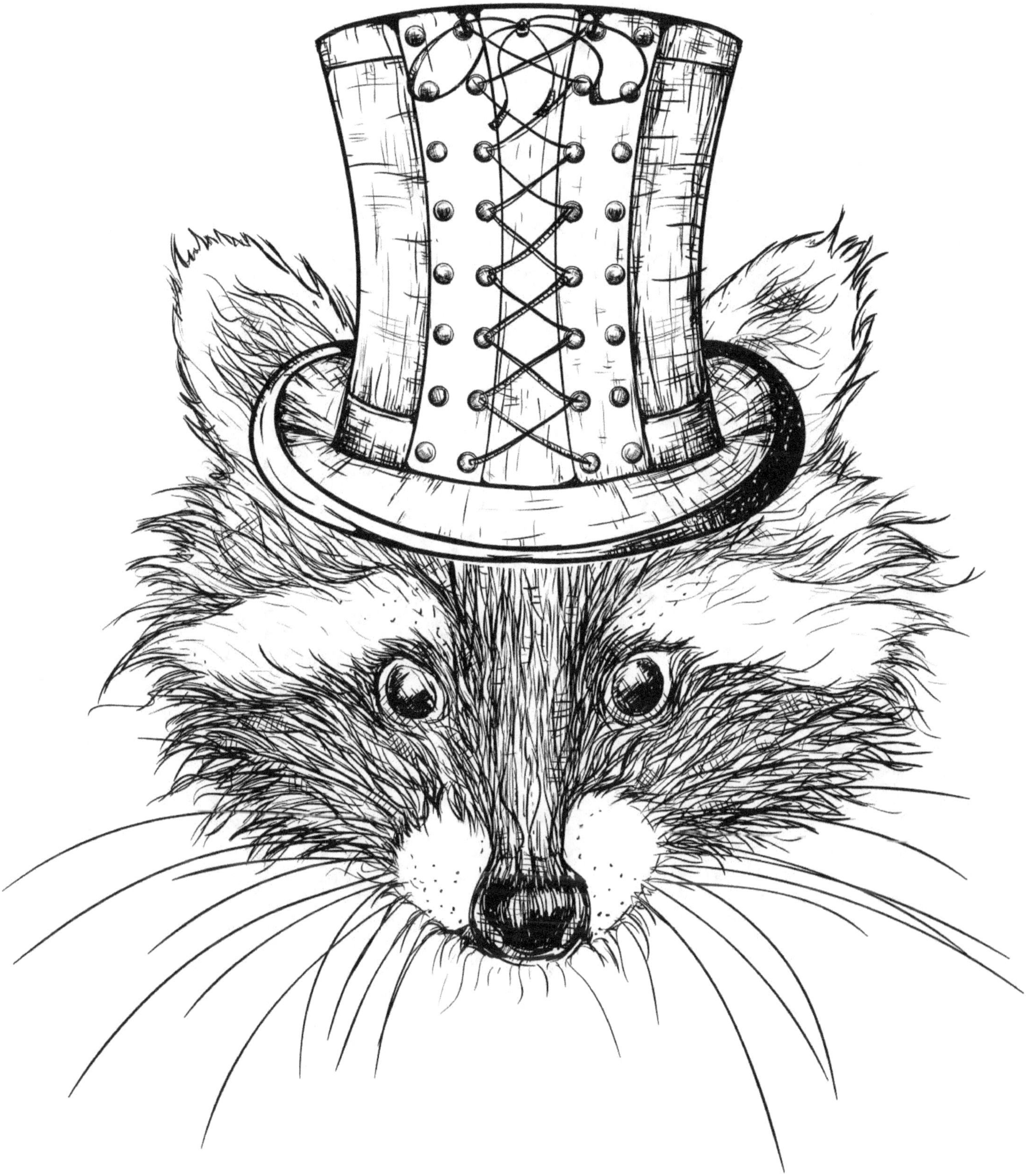

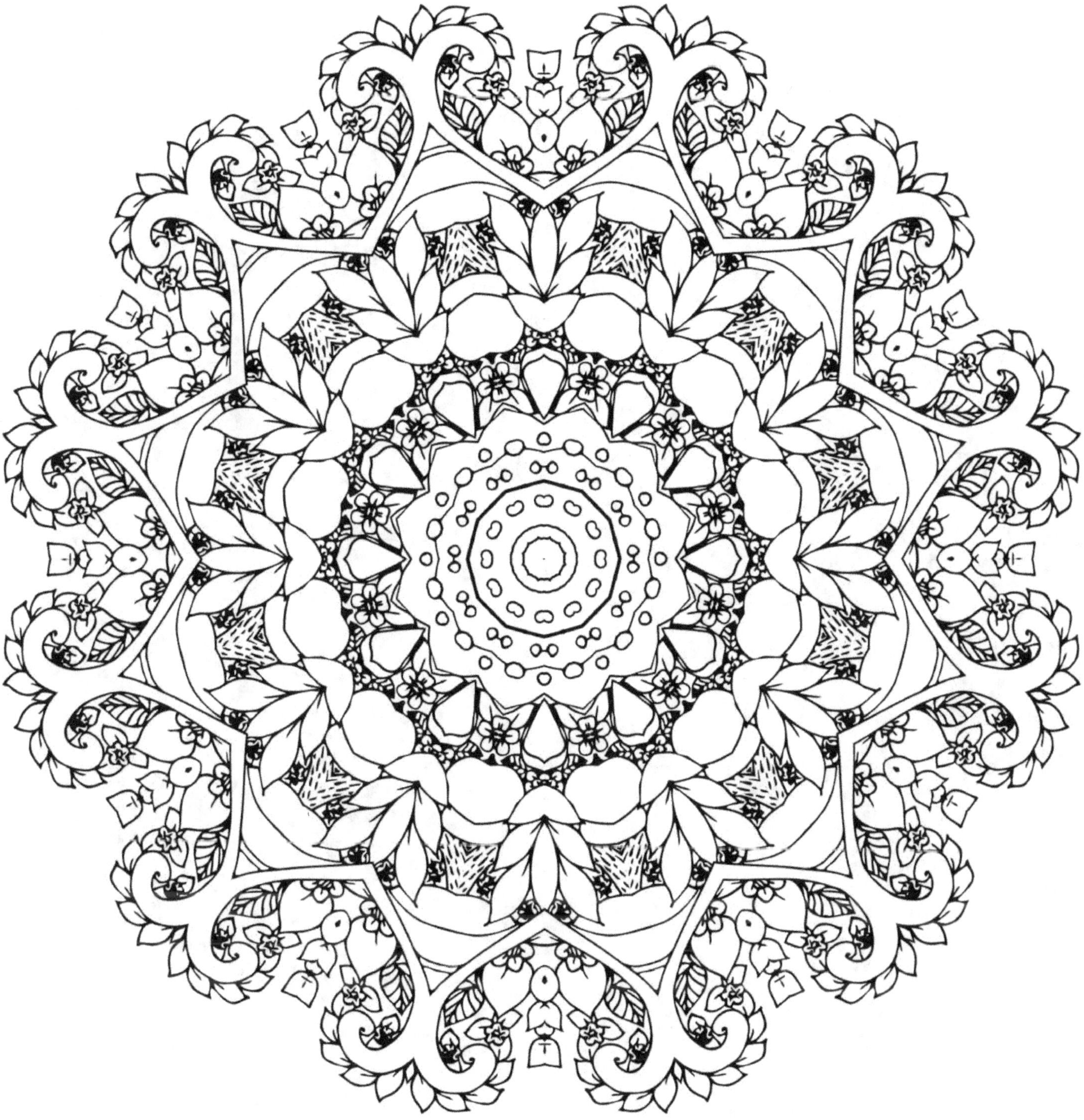

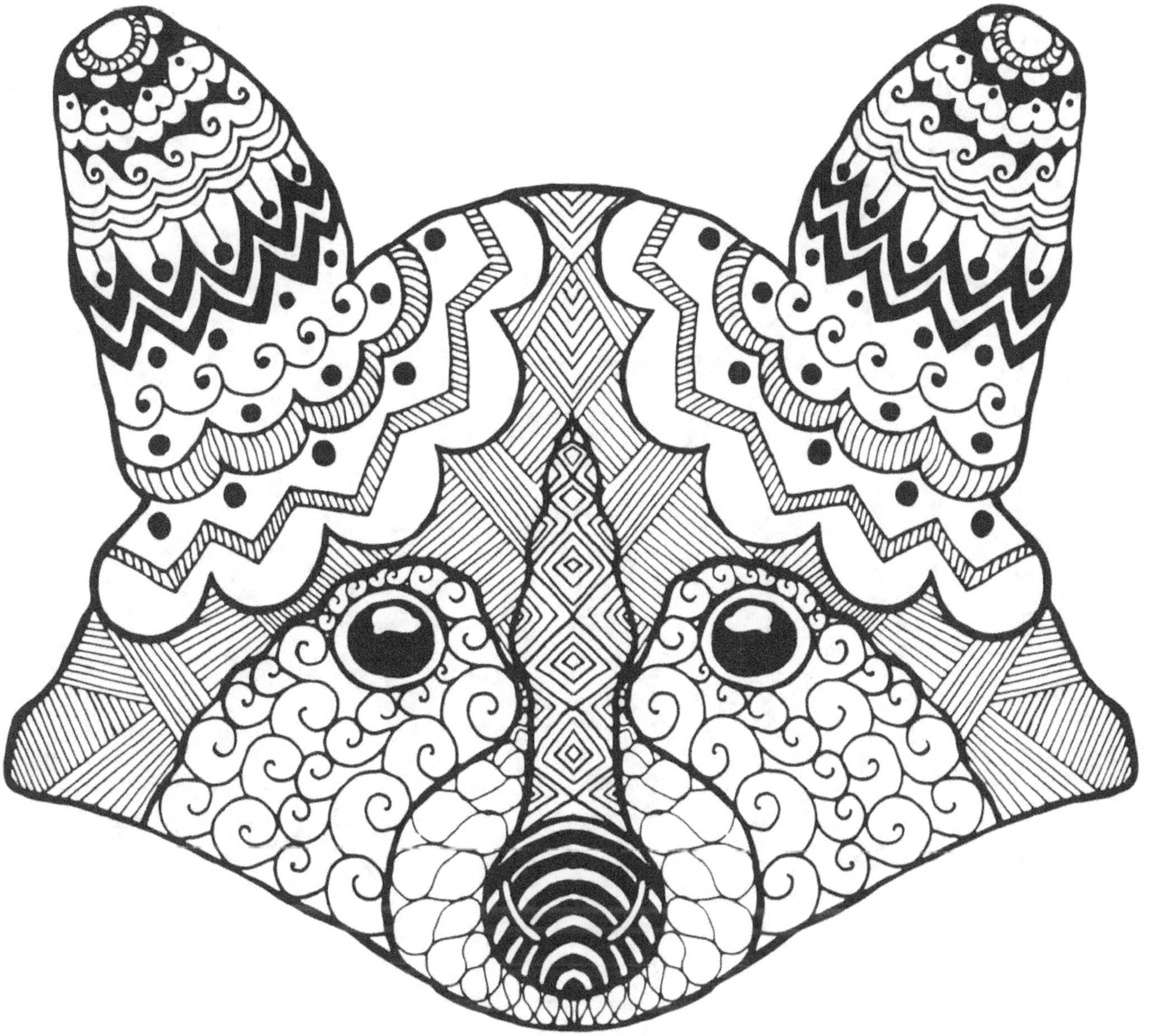

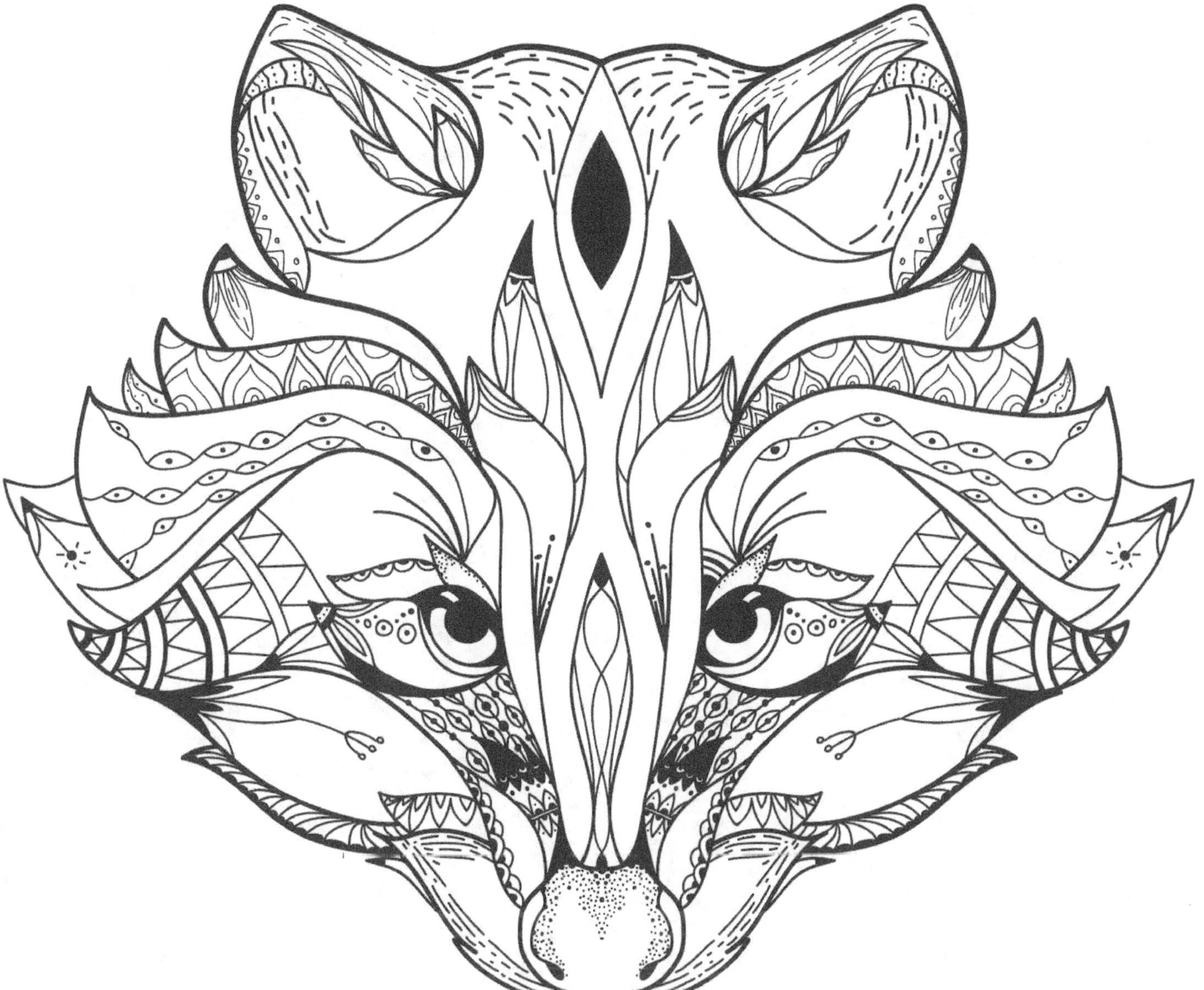

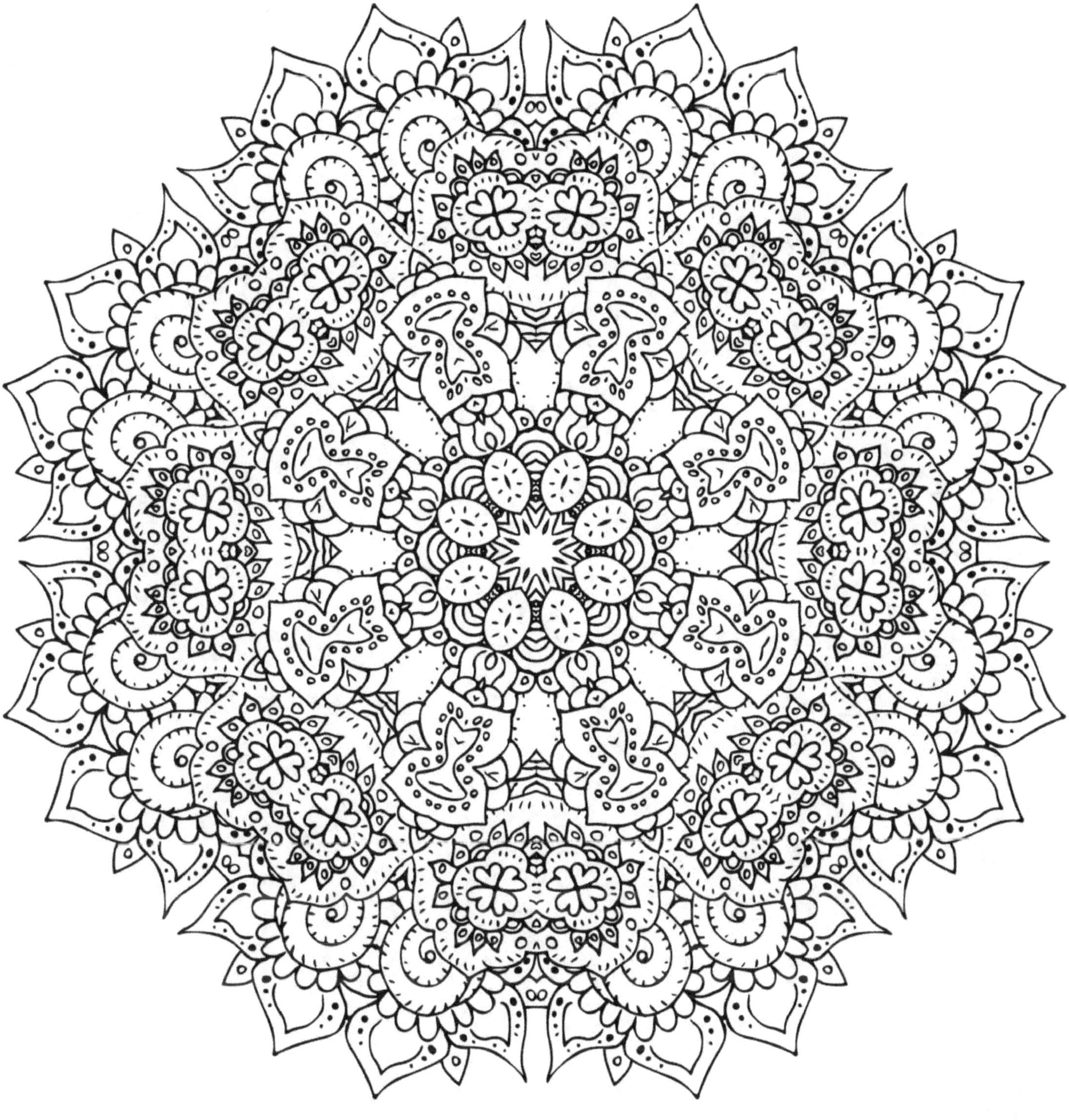

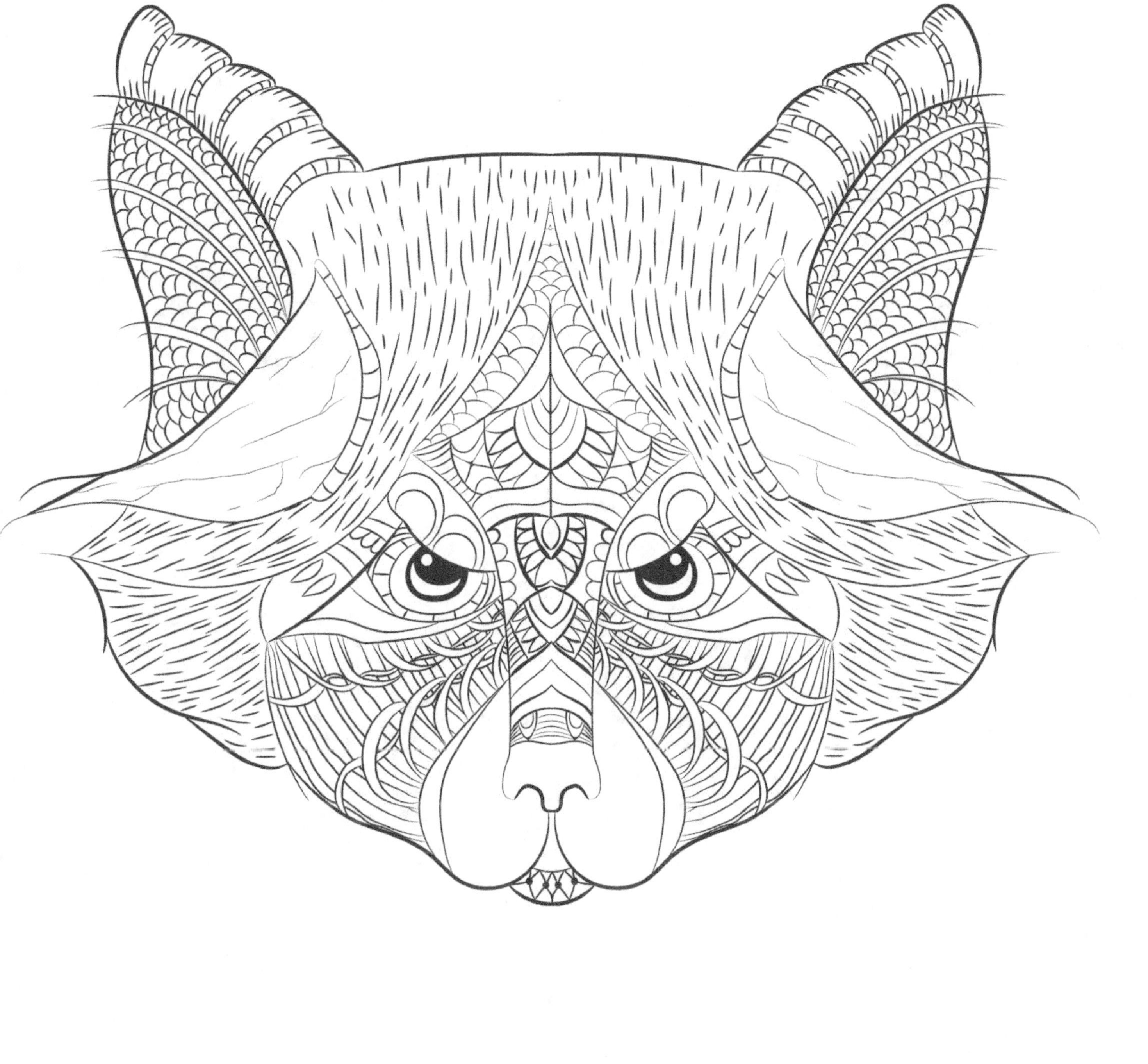

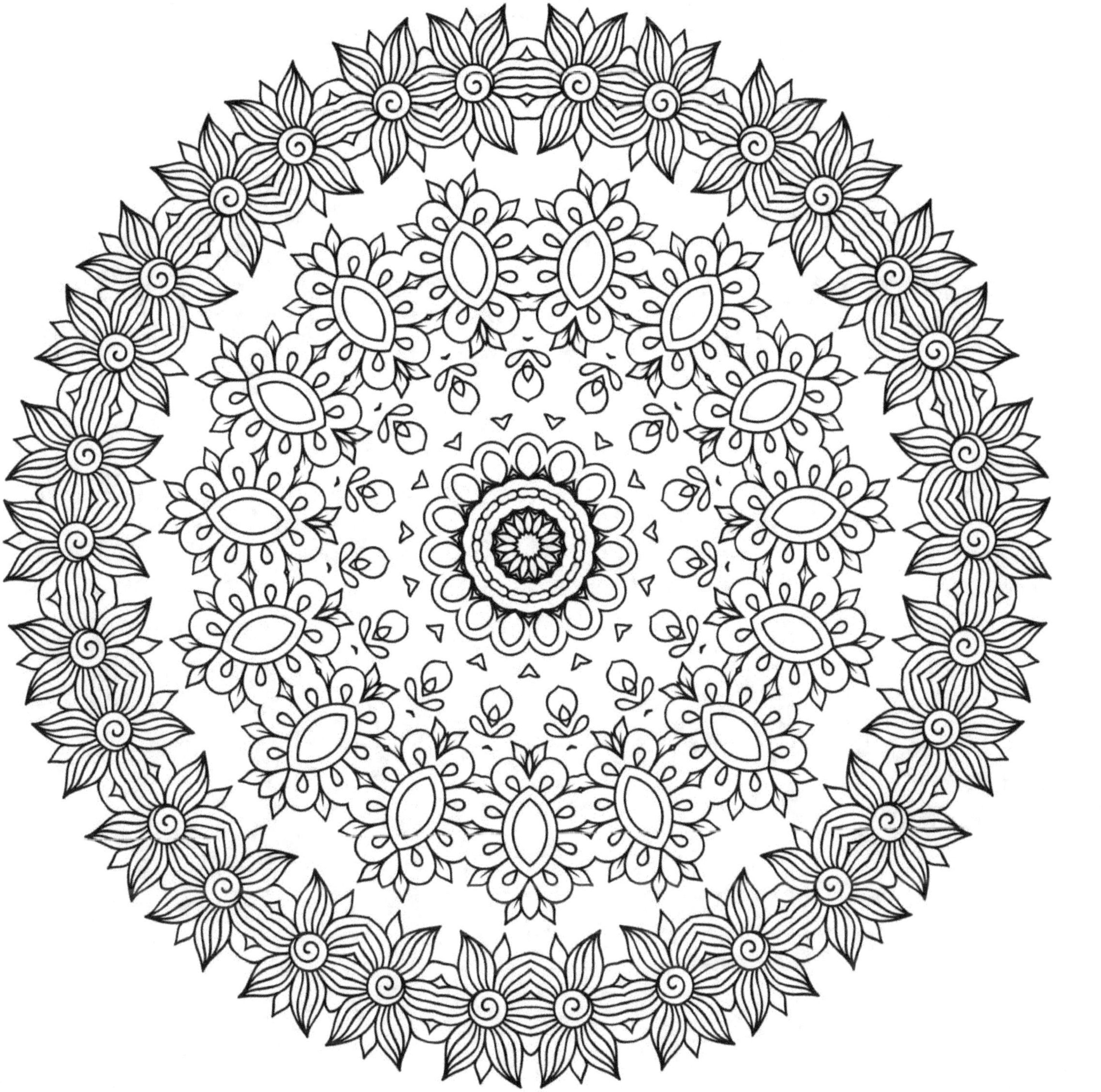

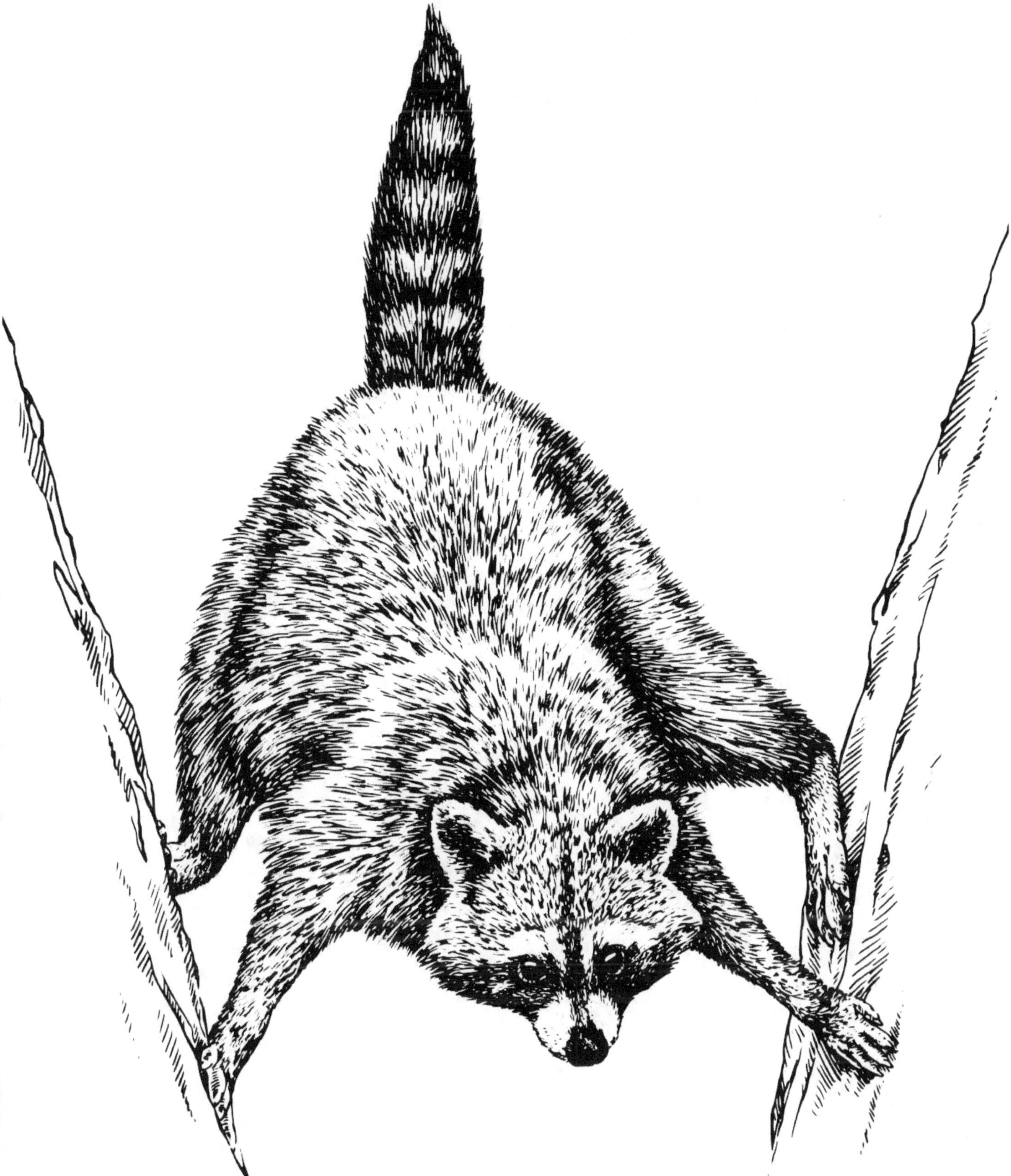

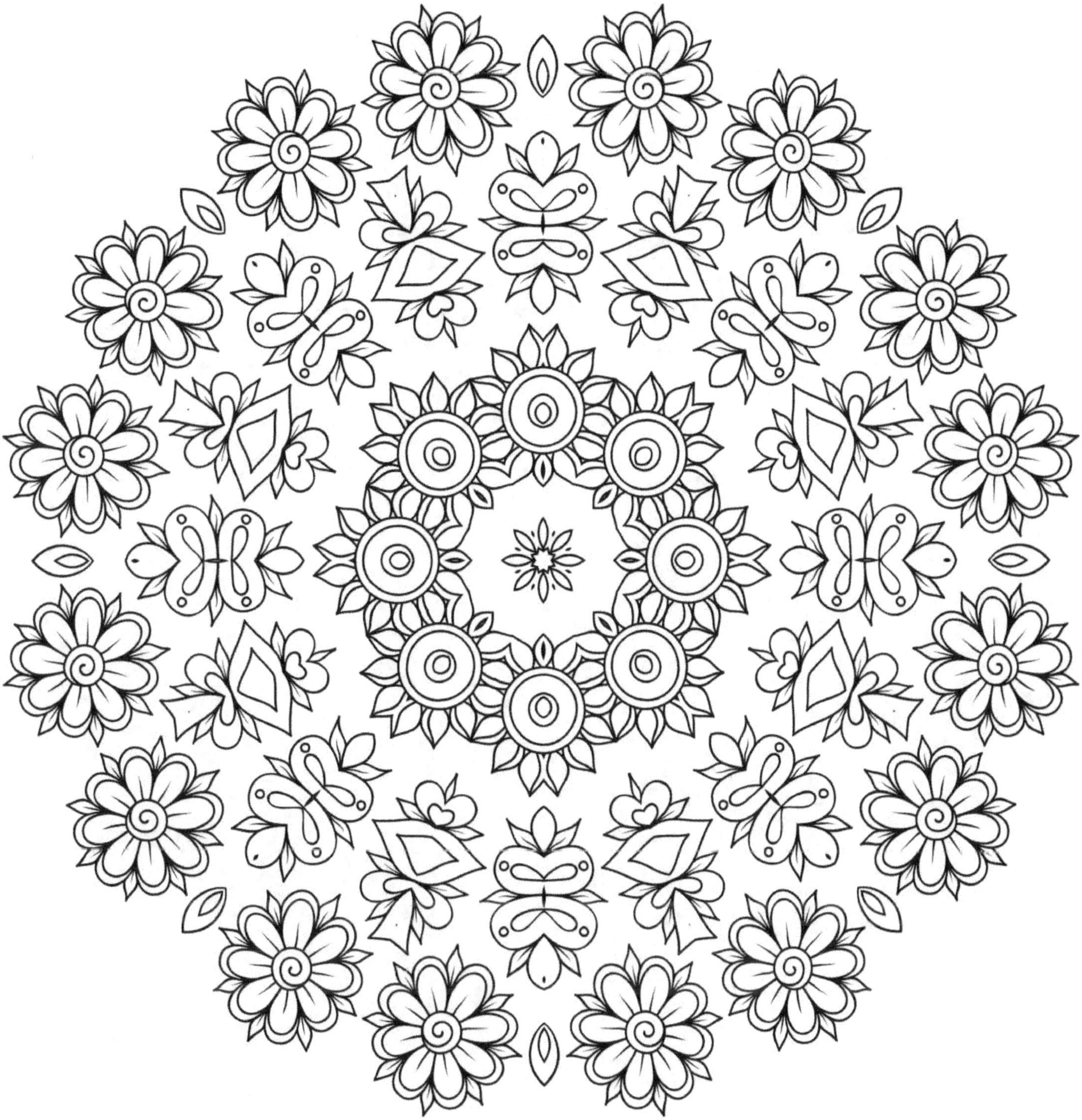

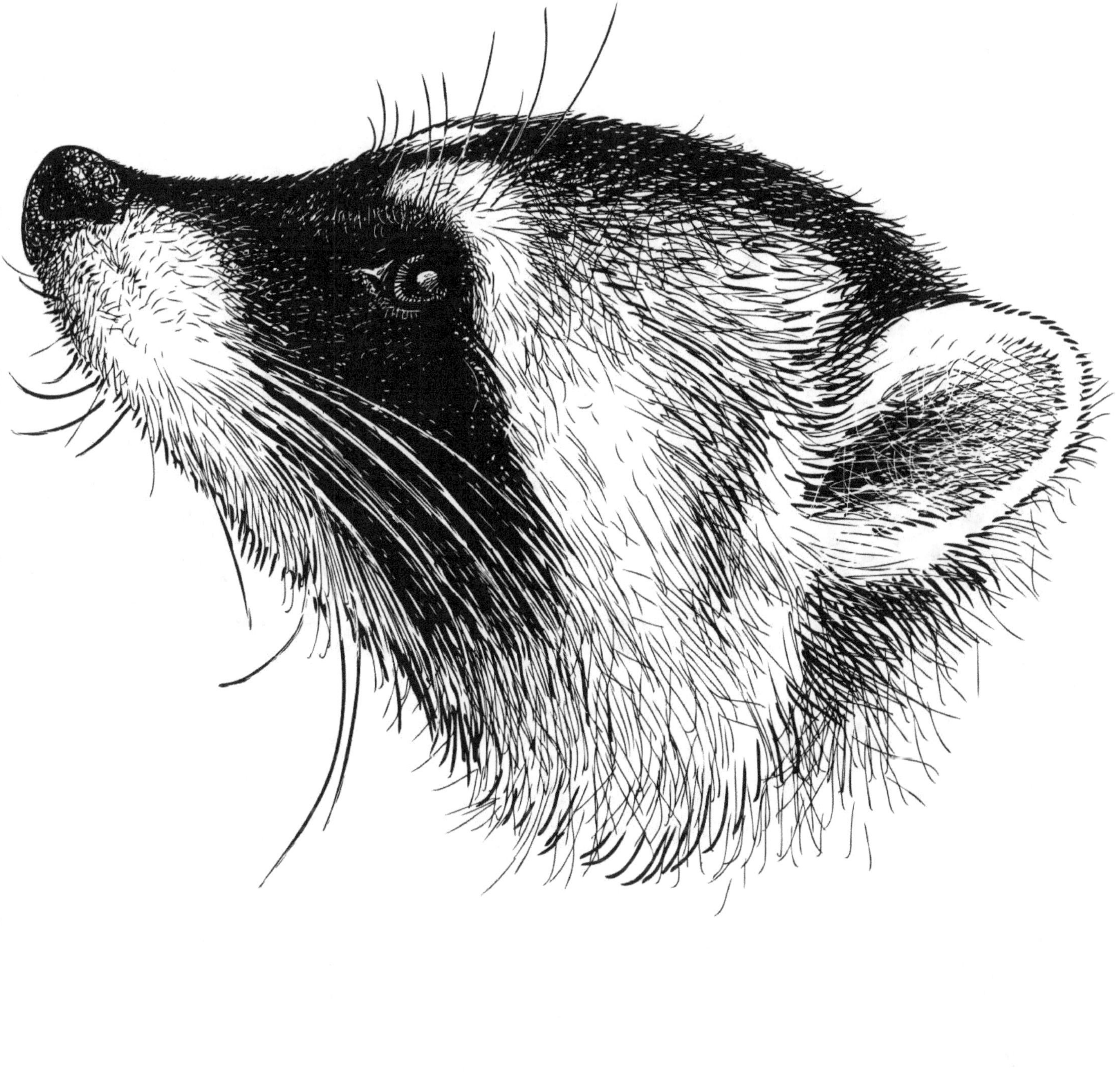

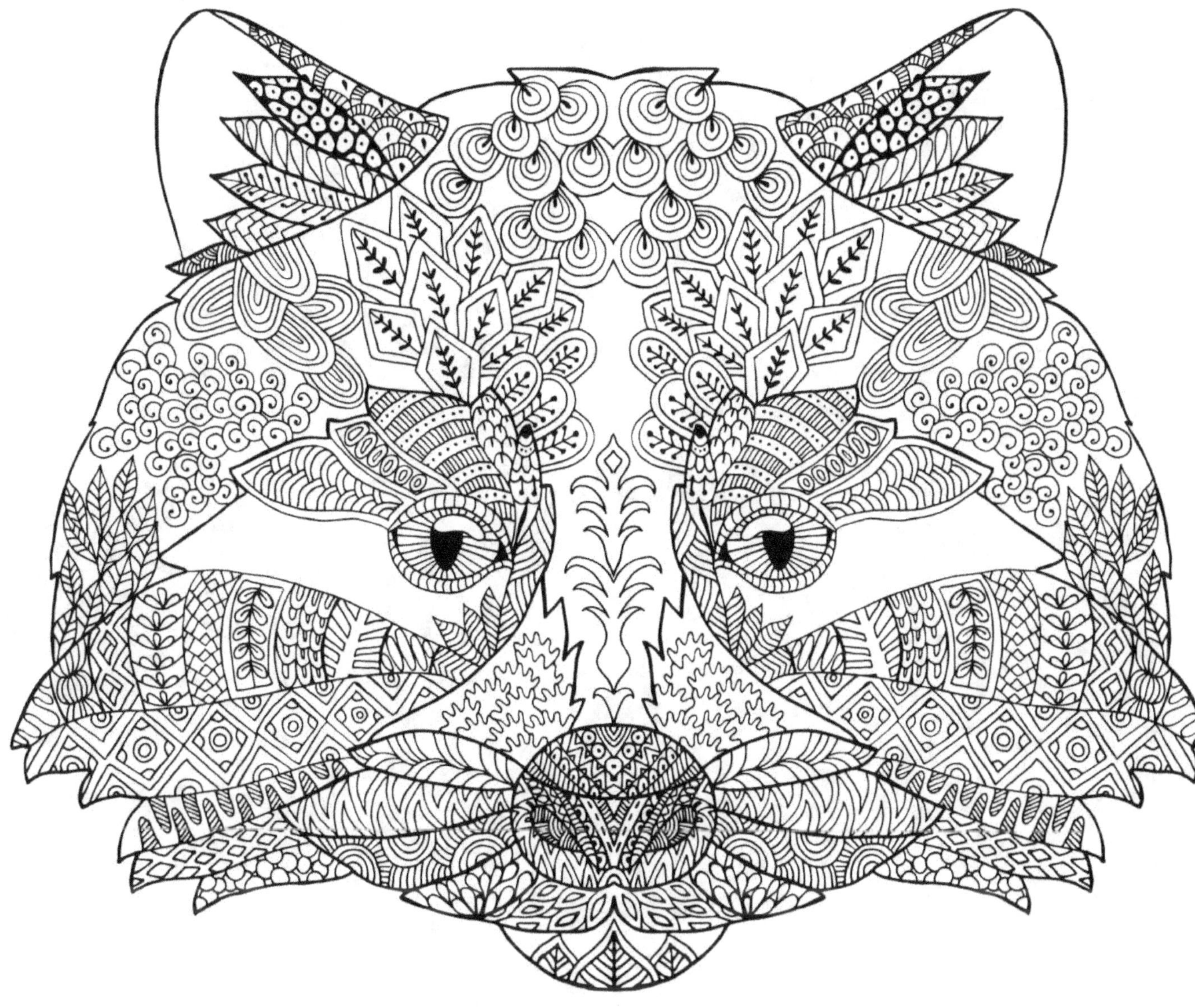

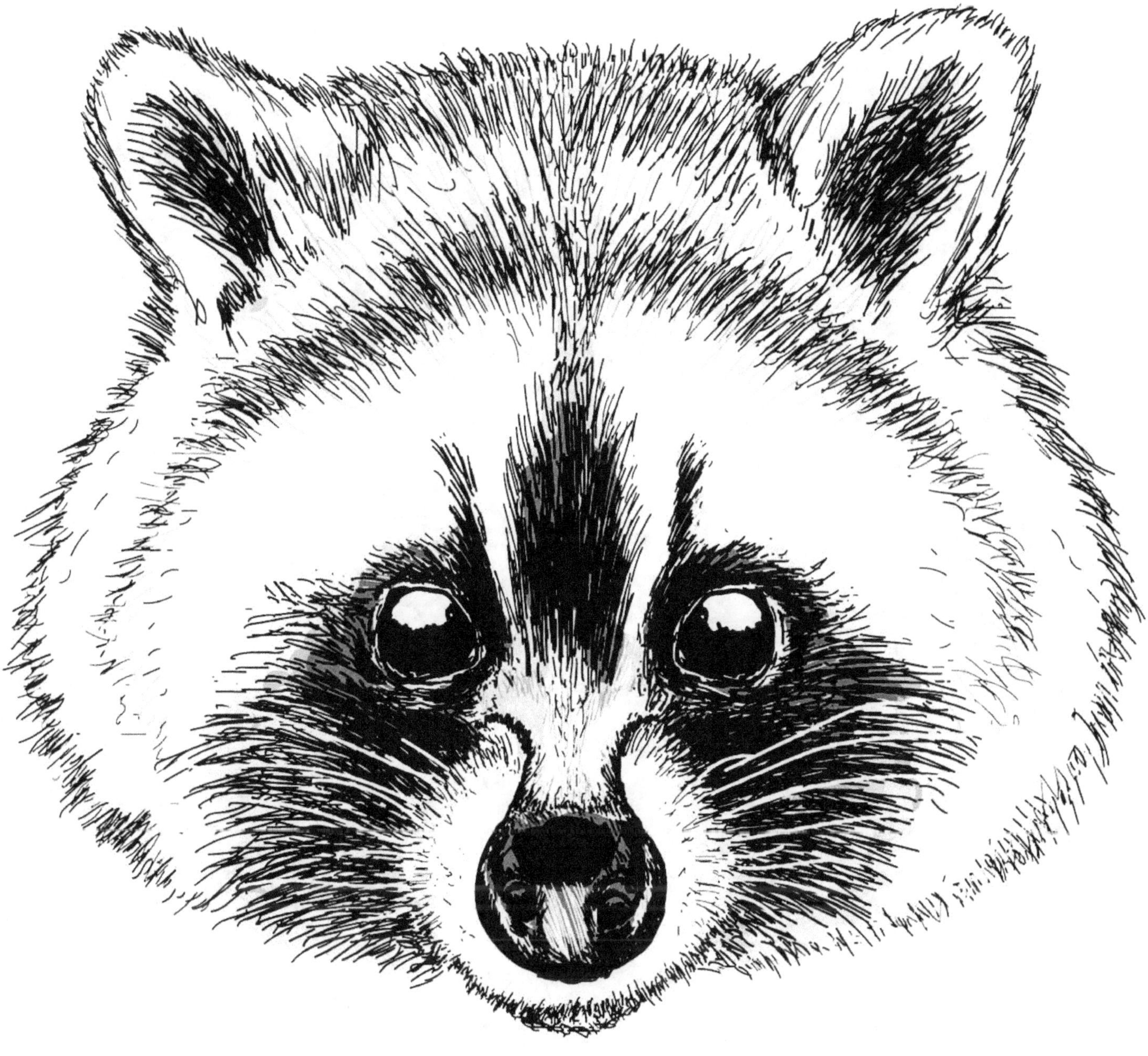

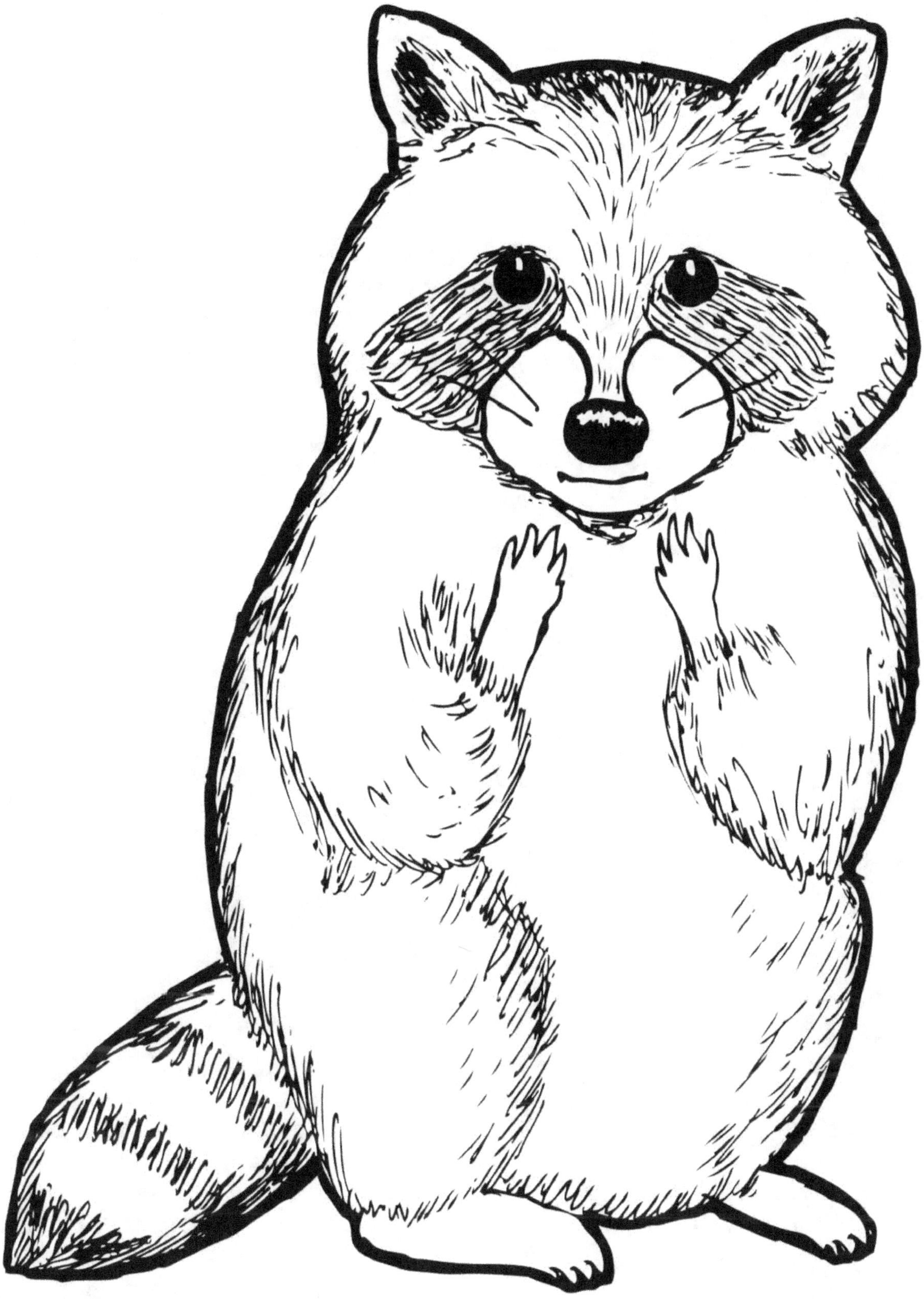

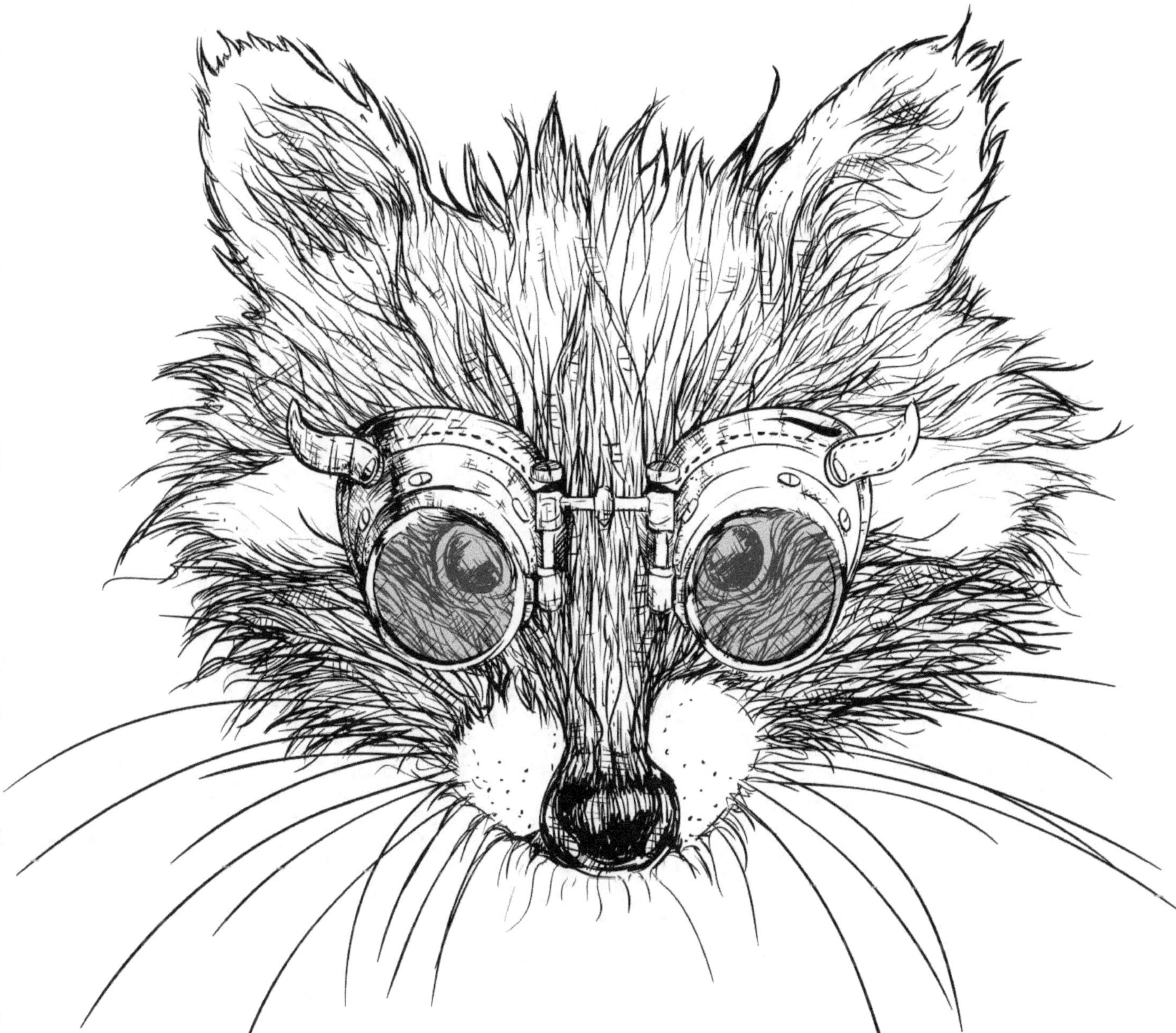

www.ingramcontent.com/pod-product-compliance
Lightning Source LLC
Chambersburg PA
CBHW081305170526
45165CB00011B/3414
9781548179786